Johanna Schär is a French and Swiss art historian specializing in photography. She won the Swiss Prize for encouraging research in art history in 2009. She has a strong interest in pictures, education and sustainability. *Pictures of women* is her first book.

To Amanda Todd,
To girls and women,
To boys and men.

Johanna Schär

PICTURES OF WOMEN: A PRACTICAL ESSAY ON PICTURES AND EDUCATION

AUSTIN MACAULEY PUBLISHERS™

LONDON • CAMBRIDGE • NEW YORK • SHARJAH

A CIP catalogue record for this title is available from the British Library.

ISBN 9781035865048 (Paperback)
ISBN 9781035865055 (ePub e-book)

www.austinmacauley.com

First Published 2024
Austin Macauley Publishers Ltd®
1 Canada Square
Canary Wharf
London
E14 5AA

20240711

I thank my mother and grandmother as well as my friends, Amandine, Noémie and Myriam. I also thank all the team of Austin Macauley Publishers.

An Environment Packed with Pictures

We, children, men, and women, are influenced by the pictures that we see every day in our environment: at home on the internet and on TV, in video games, in magazines and books, as well as on the streets on giant billboards. Pictures are now a large part of our environment; they are available everywhere. Our means of transportation, such as our buses, trams, and trains, broadcast them as well; planes do so in the air too. We are constantly surrounded and therefore bombarded by pictures, which whether we like it or not impact us and shape our perception of reality. Digital pictures get along very well with our idea of futurism and what our modern environment should look like: a high-tech urban environment packed with screens to display them. However, as more and more advanced technological devices increase the means of picture production to make them more and more available in our everyday lives, the content quality of these pictures remains low-advanced.

Influential Pictures

We are bound by the kind of pictures that restrain our perception of reality. Indeed, these pictures work as labels that shorten our understanding of the world. They limit what they depict: women and men of all ages, whatever their cultural and social backgrounds. Even animals are restricted when portrayed. Unfortunately, we cannot pass these pictures without being impressed; we cannot totally erase them from our minds once watched. These pictures root stereotypes of all sorts in our minds – that is to say mental images – without us realizing it.

Generally speaking, pictures are human productions made through technology. They are subjective constructs, so they are neither neutral nor exhaustive. They reflect what their author and producer perceive from reality and what they want to show to others. This means that all pictures go through a very selective process of the information during their making and that the quality of the pictures is dependent on their author and producer's goodwill. After their making, pictures are also selected among many others to be widely broadcast or not. Like all kinds of circulating information, they are either valued and emphasized by the media or discarded. As a result, what we see in the media is what a minority of influential people has decided to show to all others. The establishment directs the kind of pictures seen and from them molds fashions, tastes, and thoughts.

This is particularly the case of pictures of women that are spread all over the streets and on the internet: advertisements, music video clips, films, TV shows, magazines among various means of display. These pictures highly standardize the way we see women today; they focus exclusively on women's sex appeal, and in doing so, they omit to show women as complex, rich, and deeply internal human beings. They also fail to represent the diversity of women in terms of career, face, body shapes and age that exists in our society and in the world. Like adults, girls and boys are deeply influenced by these mainstream depictions of women that surround them. At home, girls tend to counterbalance their supremacy by posting online pictures of themselves little dressed or nude. Then, they can get cyberbullied because of these pictures. All of these, i.e., mainstream pictures of women and private pictures of girls, lead to severe limitations of women, which consequently restrict all human beings. As these two types of pictures are two sides of the same coin, I will address them one after another.

Pictures Used to Cyberbully Girls. Let's Talk about It. Let's Care about It

Pictures are not bad things in themselves, but they can be used in many ways, including badly to hurt people. With the rise of digital technology, pictures have become a means of communication as powerful as words; depending on the way they are used, they can have a positive or a negative impact on someone else's life. Today, pictures can be misused on the internet to blackmail or cyberbully, so to speak, to destroy someone else's public image. Children and teenage girls are particularly exposed to blackmailing and cyberbullying because they tend to overexpose themselves, especially their bodies, through pictures posted on the internet; their webcam's live images, videos and photographs are visible to all, including malicious people who can steal, misuse, or criticize them. Children and teenagers do not know yet what is privacy. It is not quite sure that adults who also spend a part of their lives on social media know either. Indeed, the birth of new means of communication on the internet, such as online chat and self-posting, has blurred fundamental limits; what is public and what is private is not so clear anymore. The growing presence of pictures that show women nude and little dressed in public – on the internet and on the streets – also contributes to blurring this fundamental limit between what can be shown publicly and what should be kept hidden. However, the boundary between public and private life still exists; respecting it remains necessary to protect oneself. Children and teens love exploring online communication; like adults, they can unpurposely blur fundamental limits, when they use webcams in their bedrooms to connect with a large and unknown audience to chat, sing, dance or seduce. By performing in public suchlike, they take their bedroom for a stage. They mix up private and public life to their own risks.

Explaining Girls, the Difference between Private and Public Life

At a time of over-self-exposition through pictures, there is an urge to teach girls to protect their privacy as soon as they can handle a webcam or a smartphone. It is important that parents set up time to give their children clear information, so to say "practical tools", about privacy. For example, we can give children some clues by asking them: "What is private?" and "What is public?". If girls learn that there is a limit between the two, they will be more able to protect their privacy. At the theatre, the artists' lodges are hidden from the public's eyes. An evening at the theatre will help children realise not everything is shown on stage: red curtains separate the stage (public and shown) from the lodges (private and hidden).

Today's Basic Toolkit for Girls Includes Talks and Clear Information about Privacy:

1. Clearing up the difference between private and public life:
   - Asking girls: "What is private?" (i.e., what belongs to you?) and "What is public?" (i.e., what belongs to you and everyone else?). What is private: their bedroom, their body. What is public: their school, the street, the internet.
   - An evening at the theatre will help girls to see the difference between the stage (public and shown) and the lodges (private and hidden).

2. Explaining girls that the internet is a public space but a virtual one:
   - Offering girls, a specific space outside their bedroom to show up online: a neutral room (free of personal belongings) or a white wall.
   - Accustoming girls to dress as much as boys with non-revealing clothes online and in public (on the street, at school): short and sexy clothes, necklines, transparent and skinny clothes overexpose girls. Revealing clothes can be worn in private (offline at home).

3. Giving girls information about private pictures:
   - Some pictures are too private to be shown online and shared with others by phones and emails, like pictures of oneself nude, topless

> and little dressed at home, at parties, on the beach or elsewhere.
> — These pictures can be stolen and misused by others, even by people we trust. Accounts on social media can be hacked.

Privacy as a Treasure

Our privacy is a treasure; it is the only thing we really possess. A treasure is something highly precious that needs to be kept hidden.

Our body and sexuality are precious; they belong to ourselves; they are not made to be shown online through pictures.

Private pictures include pictures of oneself nude, topless or little dressed at home, at parties, on the beach or elsewhere. They can be webcam's images, videos, or photographs. Private pictures should be neither posted on the internet nor shared by phones or emails. Digital images are too volatile; pictures can be easily stolen and misused also by people that we personally know and trust; they can be stored and misused years later as well. Sharing nude and sexual pictures of oneself even between partners – act referred to as "sexting" – could lead to negative outcomes if the relationship ends, such as revenge porn, sextortion, cyberbullying, and bullying. Teenagers who sext or post private pictures online are not aware of this possible backlash[*]. Providing them information on privacy and private pictures will prevent "revenge porn" –

---

[*] After Sameer Induja, "It is Time to Teach Safe Sexting", Cyberbullying Research Center, 16 January 2020: https://cyberbullying.org/it-is-time-to-teach-safe-sexting

a revenge taken by an ex-partner or a relative who posts nude or sexual pictures of a girl/boy on the internet. It will also prevent "sextortions" – blackmail conducted with nude, topless or sexual pictures to obtain further nude images, a sexual act or money. According to surveys, about 5% of middle and high school students are the target of sextortion. Sextortion can be made by a well-known ex-partner or a friend, often a teen about the same age as the victim or, more rarely, by a serial blackmailer adult who has never had any contact with the girl before[*].

One Single Topless Picture: When a Teen Becomes an Image

Online predators, such as serial blackmailers, are eager to capture nude, topless and sexual pictures on the internet to further manipulate girls. Private pictures can be traded and posted online on porn websites or sent to the girl's Facebook

---

[*] According to two surveys on sextortion conducted in 2016 and 2019, each of them based on a U.S. sample of about 5,500 middle and high school students, about 5% of the students were the target of sextortion. Most of the time the aggressor asked for more photos (38%), a sexual act (29%), or money (29%). Aggressors over 18 years old were rare (less than 5%). Surprisingly, these two surveys revealed that boys were more likely to be the target of sextortion than girls, but girls were more likely to have been sextorted by a stranger than boys. These surveys were conducted by Sameer Hinduja and Justin W. Patchin, for further details see the post written by Justin W. Patchin, "Sextortion: More Insight Into the Experiences of Youth", Cyberbullying Research Center, 19 November 2019: https://cyberbullying.org/sextortion-more-insight-into-the-experiences-of-youth

friends if she does not respond to the predator's threat. Parents and their teenagers can watch the YouTube video made by the young Amanda Todd, titled *My Story: Struggling, Bullying, Suicide, Self-Harm* (2012). It will help to open a discussion about the dangers of posting private pictures. In this video, Amanda Todd explained how she was first blackmailed with a topless picture – a screen capture made by a serial blackmailer when she was showing herself topless online via a webcam before a large and unknown audience – then cyberbullied and bullied in her school because of this picture. It is important to first ask teenagers what they feel and think about Amanda Todd's story before providing them further explanations.

The suicide Amanda Todd committed after having been publicly slashed both on social media and at her school should be said, but carefully explained to teenagers; she was endlessly both cyberbullied and bullied because of this topless picture for which she received excessively violent insults. She experienced harsh verbal attacks and endless rumors, to the point of being socially excluded. The topless picture kept being used by the blackmailer and shared on the internet without any possibility to stop its broadcast. This one single topless picture confined Amanda Todd to a narrow image that did not represent herself as a whole person – a sensitive young girl – but reduced her to a fragment of her body.

Pictures are not exhaustive; we cannot reduce somebody to an image.

This story of a misused picture could have happened to anyone: a girl or a woman, a boy, or a man. Nevertheless, pictures depicting nude, topless or little-dressed girls are more likely to be misused and shared because of the particularly high demands from boys and men.

Cyberbullying as a Viral Trend to Care

Bullying, which has taken new destructive forces on the internet through pictures and comments, should be addressed by the state. We should take care of the victims in the first place and not forget to sustain those who cyberbully and bully. For complex psychological and social reasons, these children and adults terribly lack self-esteem. Some of their basic needs are not met at home, and in school, as a result, they are frustrated and packed with anger. They feel the need to diminish others to feel better and, to do so, look to take advantage of both confident and sensitive ones. These children and adults need help to overcome this profound lack of self-esteem as well as the incredible amount of violence that it creates within themselves that they discharge on others. Punishments will never stop cyberbullying and bullying; they will never end any form of violence. We need to work on a much deeper level as well as on a national scale to do so. I have no idea how society could support adults and provide them the loving care, attention, and respect they did not receive when they were children; maybe loving care centers with intensive yoga and meditation practices could prune their old mental schemas and help them build new ones. But I do have some clues to support children of today. This goes far beyond pictures of women, but the loop is necessary.

To change the way pictures and words are used today, we need to better meet children's basic needs: to raise their self-esteem and confidence but also to allow children to express themselves. Children need to express their own personalities, i.e., their abilities, self-interests, their feelings, and thoughts, without entering competition with each other. This will help children to respect themselves and others more. Education is the key; a child-based education will fulfil every child's basic needs properly, while non-competitive group activities will enhance the group membership every school needs. Along the way, information about respect, cyberbullying, bullying and nonviolent communication will support children's social lives. In this whole process, allowing children and teenagers to connect with nature rather than technology will also be essential for their own well-being and that of the community.

A Child-Based Education to Fulfil Every Child's Basic Needs

The pedagogy of Dr Maria Montessori is among the world's most effective pedagogies for building up a benevolent classroom atmosphere. By respecting each child's learning abilities and individual interests, therefore each child's personality, this pedagogy gives children the opportunity to respect themselves and each other. This pedagogy makes children happy because it connects them to their own needs; they learn according to their own pace and choose which learning activities they want to do, without being either tested or rated. As a result, children love learning; they compare less and avoid competing. Not only they are more connected with themselves but they are also more connected with others; they show more signs of empathy and help each other more when one of them encounters difficulties in the classroom. It is then for good reason that schools inspired by the Montessori education are now flourishing around the world. Such teaching methods develop along self-esteem, confidence, and other essential human qualities, such as inner discipline, respect, mutual aid, and empathy, which naturally break down competition and reduce bullying as well as cyberbullying in the classroom. The human scale of these schools also contributes to connecting pupils together; everyone knows each other, which creates a sense of community. If not all, some of Maria Montessori's main ideas can be implemented in public and private schools by teachers and school boards. Parents and teachers can get involved by reading about it and using the philosophy of Maria Montessori at home and in schools. And for those who look for a nice job, here is the good news: there is plenty to create in education. Other child-based educations are also efficient in fulfilling children's basic needs and bond children together. A list below provides key readings that also include the references further mentioned in this chapter.

Improvisation Theatre, Yoga, Meditation and Nature to Enhance the Group Membership Every School Needs

Non-competitive group activities based on cooperation rather than competition can also be implemented in English and sports programs. Improvisation theatre games, meditation, and yoga work miracles to reduce tensions within pupils. They connect individuals to each other instead of splitting them between winners and losers like traditional school activities do. Improvisation theatre and meditation develop social skills such as mutual aid, cooperation, and empathy, while yoga brings inner peace to its practitioners. They give individuals the opportunity to express and be themselves while still being part of a group. Practitioners feel accepted the way they are, and as a result, they respect each other more. These activities require almost no equipment, and for this reason, they are inexpensive and thus eco-friendly. Yoga and meditation can also be practiced at no cost in a nearby park or in a lush nature; this will increase their positive effects on the group.

Indeed, allowing children and teenagers to connect to nature is another efficient way to release their stress and pacify the whole group. At school, straight observation of nature in the playground and school's surroundings can be conducted on a regular basis in natural science and art classes. Insects, animals, trees, stones, river, sky, and clouds can be observed through magnifying lenses or sketches. As technology is everything these days, children and teens like adults must learn to restore balance in their lives by strengthening their relationship with their natural surroundings; it is essential for their own well-being and that of the community. It will give children and teens the ability to balance their strong taste for technology and unplug from technological devices when they need it. "Unplugging": this underestimated skill is of vital importance to protect oneself in cases of cyberbullying. Practicing it at school and at home can save lives. Nature itself provides a safe environment children and teens can rely on when their social lives go rough online.

At Home
Unplugging for a Day
(Once a Week or a Month)

All smartphones, computers, TV remote controls and other technological devices from parents, their children and guests will be turned off and kept out of reach and sight in a specific drawer one day a week or a month, for example, on Sundays.

- This is much easier to start when the weather is good enough to go outside (in spring or in the summer) and when children are young. Teens may offer strong resistance at the beginning. A democratic vote will help to involve them. Each family member can bring their own ideas to organize this day.
- At the very beginning, it is important adults bring alluring alternatives to technological devices: outdoors activities teens may love doing, like climbing a mountain to get a wonderful view, walking along a beautiful river or coast, biking around a lake, hunting for a four-leaf clover, going strawberry

> picking, enjoying restful time in nature with a picnic, books, and some drawing materials, spending a day in a park or at a festival.
> – Their friends can be invited for more fun. They will learn to unplug too.

Information about Respect, Cyberbullying, Bullying and Nonviolent Communication to Support Children's Social Life

Reading *The Universal Declaration of Human Rights* (1948) in classrooms is a good way to introduce the notion of respect every child needs to know to steer clear of cyberbullying and bullying. As this text was written after World War II to remind us to respect each other, it can be read in history and philosophy classes to speak openly about respect in past and present time with students. Another way to grow respect in children and teens' daily lives is to give them the opportunity to experience it, for example, by giving students free time and space to self-organize a one-day "festival for peace and respect" in the school with shared homemade pastries, a film screening, restful time, cooperative games or whatever they want to do all together. Such a cooperative event will be nice, especially if one of the students is cyberbullied or bullied.

Informative workshops on cyberbullying and bullying held by psychologists or other professionals in classrooms will go deeper into the subject; children and teenagers need to hear more about their spread existences, share their personal experiences and most importantly express their fears. Along these, key information about nonviolent communication, such as developed by Dr Marshall B. Rosenberg in his book *Nonviolent Communication: A Language of Life* (2015), can be taught through role-playing games; they are the basics everyone needs to run through life. Dr Marshall B. Rosenberg's book can also be read and discussed by high school students in English classes. His idea of nonviolence comes from Gandhi, who inspired him. A screening of the film *Gandhi* (1982) about Gandhi's life can both show students how violence engenders violence and how nonviolence can end it. Teaching nonviolent communication skills will impact all children and teenagers deeply; they will be able to better communicate with others without hurting them, then words like pictures will not be so misused.

A Text to Teenagers: How to Close Up Pictures Used to Cyberbully Girls

As cyberbullying has become viral these last few years, hurting many girls, here is what we can do to protect girls: **Not watching topless, nude, sexual pictures used to cyberbully girls**. There are much nicer things to do, like going to the movies or visiting an art museum with a girlfriend.

Deleting these pictures. If you receive one, it is wise to delete it and not reply, even if it is sent by a close friend. This silence gives the message: "I'm not interested in this." If your friend complains, you can explain to her or him that you feel uncomfortable receiving these kinds of pictures and that you prefer to receive pictures that do not hurt anyone.

Sharing and speaking about nice pictures that do not hurt anyone with friends and schoolmates to avoid spreading the word and making things worse if a girl is cyberbullied.

Remembering that we have the right to stand up not only to defend our own rights but also to defend those of others. If you see something wrong, like one of your schoolmates is cyberbullied, and you can do something, even a tiny little thing, it will help her a lot. It does not matter if this girl is a friend or a stranger, everyone deserves respect. This is a fundamental human right written in *The Universal Declaration of Human Rights* (1948):

"Everyone has the right to life, liberty and security of person." (Article 3)

"No one shall be subjected to torture or to cruel, inhuman or degrading treatment or punishment." (Article 5)

Cyberbullying and bullying are both cruel and degrading punishments. Even if the girl has made a mistake, it does not mean that she deserves to be punished for it. Despite her mistake, she deserves to be respected like everyone else.

Tiny little things that will help this girl: sharing and speaking about nice pictures with friends and schoolmates, telling this girl a nice word such as "I'm sorry for all what people do to you, you don't deserve it" or inviting her if you throw a party.

Freedom of the Viewer

Intentions and values matter even through pictures. The internet acknowledges a fundamental human right by providing us with boundless freedom of expression; however, it is not a reason to use this fundamental human right to be mean and hurt others with pictures and comments. Even an apparently funny image can be offensive and considered as cyberbullying. As a viewer, we can do much to close these kinds of pictures and others used to cyberbully girls – topless, nude, sexual pictures. Let's watch out for the kind of pictures that we use to feed our mind and soul with; we can choose to click or not on that video or watch this picture rather than this one. We are also free to click off or press delete. It is up to each of us to watch and share pictures that do not hurt or insult anyone else.

In Case of Cyberbullying

As the internet is everywhere in our daily lives, a girl who is cyberbullied does not feel safe anywhere, not even at home. Severe cyberbullying and bullying have already led many girls to commit suicide. Parents need to act quickly to relieve their child's distress, for example:

- Being there for the child without judging or punishing:

    - Listening to her fears, feelings, and needs; if she cannot find the words, she can either draw, dance or write a diary to express herself daily.

    - Chatting with her regularly to stay connected with what's going on in her life.

- Getting and providing her information about cyberbullying:

    - The Cyberbullying Research Centre:

http://cyberbullying.org/ is full of tips for parents, educators, and teens.

- Aija Mayrock, *The Survival Guide to Bullying: Written by a Teen*, New York, Scholastic, 2015. Aija Mayrock's own experience of bullying and cyberbullying has already helped many other girls to see that solutions exist and a full recovery is possible.
- The song *Clay* (2016) by Grace VanderWaal can help girls to get stronger.

– Reducing the time that she spends online by filling up her timetable with moments when she can feel safe and unplugged activities that she loves doing:

- Long walks or activities in nature (see also "At Home: Unplugging for a Day").
- Yoga, dance, and meditation classes can heal her pain.
- Activities with safe friends and relatives (meals and parties at home, classes, and social clubs to practice her favorite hobbies).
- Other unplugged activities (travelling, visiting art museums, drawing, reading

comforting books, watching heart-warming and funny films with happy endings)

- Asking for explicit help from her school principal, a mental health professional and, in case of a physical threat, the police.

If the girl does not get better, consider living off-grid for a year close to nature in the countryside without internet access or mobile phones.

Reading List
Key References to Develop
an Education Based on
Respect, Personal
Growth and Cooperation

To better understand children's needs, a national survey that asks every 5 to 10 years each citizen aged 5–18 years these basic questions would be necessary:

1. What do you love to do in your everyday life?
2. What would you love to do to make the world a better place?
3. What would you love to learn?

In the meantime, parents and teachers can directly ask these questions to children and teenagers to figure out and further develop their interests and talents.

The Basics of Life

As every child has different needs, interests and skills, the same school programmes for everyone cannot be relevant. However, the basics of life deserve to be taught to everyone:

expressing one's opinion, counting, and reading, as well as fundamentals that will help children to grow their body, mind, and soul throughout their lives. For example[†]:

- Yoga and meditation practices
- Nonviolent communication and cooperative activities: role-playing games, improvisation theatre, cooking and cleaning the classroom all together
- Free and spontaneous self-expression: free play, drawing, dance, personal writing, independent reading, or handicrafts
- Eco-responsibility: respecting the Earth, using environmentally friendly resources, gardening and exploring the outdoors
- Introduction to human rights and the rights of living things
- First-aid training
- Fundamentals of survival skills: building a shelter, making a fire, finding water and edible wild plants[**]
- Skills to cook healthy
- Principles of human physiology to understand how the body functions, especially when it gets sick and is injured. Information about the most common diseases as well as ways to prevent them

---

[†] Information that is no longer relevant must be updated according to changes in the society.

[**] After Hugh McManners, *The Commando Survival Manual*, London, Dorling Kindersley, 1994.

- Information about drugs and alcohol use and addictions: their physiological effects on the body and brain, health risks, advices to reduce these risks
- Information about birth control methods
- Free time to create a personal project and find a vocation
- Basic knowledge of languages spoken in neighboring countries (based on phrasebooks, grammatical bases, and conjugation of main verbs)
- A list of essential self-help books and autobiographies written by various spiritual leaders and inspirational people (Mother Teresa, Thich Nhat Hanh, Louise Hay, Gandhi, Maria Montessori, Nelson Mandela, Matthieu Ricard, Henry David Thoreau, Eckhart Tolle, Etty Hillesum and Helen Keller, among others)

Human Cooperation

If we consider that the teaching of history also belongs to the basics of life, then our view of history deserves to be revised; violence, wars, dominance and competition could certainly be taught to learn from our failures and move forward—wars could be studied to understand how conflicts arise and how to resolve them through nonviolence and negotiation–, but history classes should first show children and teenagers human cooperation around the world and men and women ingenuity through intellectual, spiritual, artistic, scientific, social and sustainable breakthroughs and inspirational projects. The biological and cultural diversity of human beings in today's world, including its religious diversity, also merits to be shown, explained, and experienced to be acknowledged as a fact. As in the Freinet pedagogy, students could use emails to communicate with students from other classrooms abroad – for example, in Mexico, in Ghana, or in China – to experience the world's cultural diversity.

The Main Issue of Today: Ecology and Sustainability

The basics of life also need to address the main issues of our time to give children information and tools to help them to cope with their environment once they are adults. Today, the environmental issue is the main issue to address in schools: how can we live a 100% sustainable life at home and at work? This is a vital question to tackle if we want to solve the environmental crisis. It would make sense to create an ecology and sustainability course that would be equally important to English and science courses. Other main issues are: how to find inner peace in our everyday life and how to share our resources and skills to give food, a shelter, clothes, medical care, and an education to everyone on earth. Gender equality is also at stake here.

The Montessori Education

Maria Montessori, *The Secret of Childhood*, Laren, The Netherlands, Montessori-Pierson Publishing Company, 2018.

Maria Montessori was a doctor and an educator who devoted her life to children's education. As she went through two world wars, she worked for human development and peace. This classic provides essential clues to understand and respond to children's needs at home and in school. The Association Maria Montessori Internationale (AMI) provides a list of training centers that offer workshops, short courses, and diploma courses: http://ami-global.org/

Céline Alvarez, *The Natural Laws of the Child*, the official website: https://www.celinealvarez.org/?locale=en

Céline Alvarez is a renowned French kindergarten teacher who has developed the work of Maria Montessori with the latest scientific findings, especially in neuroscience. Her website provides a lot of practical information and videos that show how effective this pedagogy is.

Further References on Child-Based Education

A. S. Neill, *Summerhill School: A New View of Childhood*, New York, St Martin's Griffin, 1992, p. 1–151.

A. S. Neill was the founder of Summerhill School, a self-governing and democratic school well-known for the freedom to live, play and learn that it gives to its pupils. In this bestseller, A. S. Neill shows parents and teachers how violence arises in children from unhappiness and how freedom to be themselves, good food and fresh air bring good health to children. Summerhill School was founded in 1921 and is still there. It is now run by A. S. Neill's daughter, Zoë Neill Readhead. http://www.summerhillschool.co.uk/

L'école Buissonnière (1949), a fictional film by Jean-Paul Le Chanois, is about the achievements of the revolutionary pedagogue Célestin Freinet (French audio only). It shows Freinet's pedagogical method while portraying a vivid and cooperative classroom based on pupils' interests.

Ken Robinson, *The Element: How Finding Your Passion Changes Everything*, London, Penguin Books, 2009.

Ken Robinson was a leading voice for radical change in education. In this book, he goes through a wide range of artists, scientists, athletes, business leaders and academics' life paths to explain that finding our element – nourishing our passion and individual talents – is a key to release our human potential.

André Stern, *Yo Nunca Fui a La Escuela*, Albuixech, Litera Libros, 2013.

André Stern is the son of the pedagogue Arno Stern, whose work aims to support child development, its autonomy and spontaneous creativity. André Stern has never been in school or been homeschooled. He is now a musician, composer, luthier, author, journalist, and co-director of a theatre. His testimony offers refreshing ways to think about child development and education outside of a curriculum, stress, and competition. This book is also available in French, German and Polish.

Reconnecting Children with Nature

Richard Louv, *Last Child in the Woods: Saving Our Children from Nature-Deficit Disorder*, Chapel Hill, Algonquin Books of Chapel Hill, 2008.

In this bestseller, Richard Louv shows how essential nature is for child development. The book also includes a list of actions that parents and educators can take to promote nature, from nature activities for kids to ways to promote natural school reform.

Mindfulness Meditation

The Altruism Revolution (2016), a documentary film by Sylvie Gilman and Thierry Vincent de Lestrade about altruism and meditation, demonstrates the efficiency of meditation when implemented in kindergartens and primary schools.

Eline Snel, *Sitting Still Like a Frog: Mindfulness Exercises for Kids (and Their Parents)*, foreword by Jon Kabat-Zinn, Boulder, Shambhala Publications, 2013.

Eline Snel is a therapist and certified mindfulness trainer who has been developing mindfulness meditation courses for children and teenagers. This practical book provides exercises for children (5–10 years old) and their parents, which can also be used by teachers to reduce tensions and anxiety in schools. Eline Snel gives mindfulness training courses.

http://www.elinesnel.com/

Improvisation Theatre

Keith Johnstone, *Impro: Improvisation and the Theatre*, New York, Bloomsbury, 2016. Keith Johnstone was first a schoolteacher before becoming a trainer for actors in a theatre studio. This practical book provides exercises that can be used either by English teachers to turn their classroom into a cooperative group or by parents with drama talent and actors to launch workshops in schools. Here is Keith Johnstone's website: https://www.keithjohnstone.com/

Nonviolent Communication

Gandhi (1982) is a fictional film by Richard Attenborough about the nonviolent life of Gandhi.

Marshall B. Rosenberg, *Nonviolent Communication: A Language of Life*, Encinitas, PuddleDancer Press, 2015.

Marshall B. Rosenberg was the founder of nonviolent communication. This practical book describes how to apply nonviolent communication in daily life while providing tools to improve the reader's communication skills. Both adults and high school students will benefit from its reading. The Centre for Nonviolent Communication offers nonviolent communication training courses and the possibility to hire certified trainers. https://www.cnvc.org/

Cyberbullying and Bullying

Amanda Todd (TheSomebodytoknow), *My Story: Struggling, Bullying, Suicide, Self-Harm* (2012), YouTube video.

The Cyberbullying Research Centre: http://cyberbullying.org/ is full of up-to-date information and tips for educators, parents, and teens about cyberbullying, bullying and sextortion.

Aija Mayrock, *The Survival Guide to Bullying: Written by a Teen*, New York, Scholastic, 2015.

Aija Mayrock experienced bullying and cyberbullying for several years. She wrote this self-help book to help other children and teenagers get through this experience. This book was vetted by Deborah Temkin, PhD, an expert in the field of bullying, and by psychotherapist Myrna Fleishman, PhD.

More Pictures about Women? Yes, but Please Fair and Inspiring Ones

Pictures used to cyberbully girls are not the only ones that restrict them. Other kinds of pictures shrink girls' lives.

Catchy Pictures of Women

Today, young girls have not much choices than dreaming of becoming a top model, an actress or a singer. These are stereotyped ambitions that circulate through pictures and a wide range of media, such as the internet, TV, cinema, and photography, which spread them for the good sake of the economy. These pictures of successful top models, actresses and singers are pretty much everywhere in a girl's life. Rather than girls, they benefit various businesses: advertisement, big investors, such as fashion and cosmetics industries, TV, and film productions and, finally, the music industry.

These pictures mainly depict little-dressed women whose fashion style and sometimes hot poses borrow from porn pictures to make them catchier. Among these pictures, music video clips on the internet top all the other ones because of their ability to "sell" for free not only the music but also the girl dancing in them; they are the most widespread and restrictive pictures of women. Even though these female performers personify the girl power of today, showing obvious business skills along with some artistic talents, I still want to tell them, "Put something on baby" or "Twerking sucks".

As these pictures of female performers are praised by society, girls are deeply influenced by them. Certain girls model their fashion styles and hot poses – especially twerking – online. The young Amanda Todd, who showed herself topless online, embodies the fragility of today's girls. Besides the screen capture for which she got severely cyberbullied and bullied, she posted several videos of herself singing as she dreamt of being a singer. Like other girls of her generation, she was influenced by the mainstream pictures of women that received millions of views on the internet and are, for this reason, considered the norm. It is then striking, but not surprising, if she and other teens undress online. Indeed, these pictures of little dressed girls and women have one thing in common: they both aim to attract attention, which means, in our society, to get more viewers and "likes". These two kinds of pictures are two sides of the same coin, but the slice of the coin remains thick, and a major difference divides its two sides: while female performers gain phenomenal success around the world thanks to these pictures, teens get severely cyberbullied because of them.

Let's make a point here: some people may think that these pictures of women performers are legitimate. They would embody the sexual freedom that was expected in the 1960s. If that is freedom, why not release men too? On the exact contrary to women, men are dressed from neck to toes; they are waiting for decades to get unleashed. Is it only possible to imagine a male version of the sexy performances that women do? A man could not act so in public without embarrassing himself. Men have had it for a long time: their bodies and sexuality belong to themselves; they are private. That's why men rarely show themselves nude or little dressed in public, and this picture fails to appear in our imaginations. So, here is the point: if we cannot even visualize a man entertaining the world suchlike, why do we still expect women to do so?

Even if these female performers decide to present themselves this way on stage, building up a worldwide reputation as a singer requires to get undressed. It is expected, valorized, and encouraged by the music business. The backgrounds used to set up songs reveal this intention; the beach, the swimming pool or the bed seem to naturally justify the presence of little-dressed women in video clips. Getting undressed is expected of all women whose primary work lies in showing up publicly, not only singers but also top models and actresses. It is hard not to notice how rarely they are invited to wear a loose pant. These pictures seal the social pact made between women and the music, fashion, cosmetics, film, and TV industries; women must accept it to get a chance to launch a career.

We should look at actresses, top models, and singers differently. Who knows if these overexposed women do not feel restricted by their images?

The Iconic Marilyn Monroe: When a Woman Becomes an Image

The iconic Marilyn Monroe, who knew better than anyone else how to act in front of a camera, was also one of its greatest victims. Indeed, she was very limited by the kinds of roles that Hollywood proposed to her that bound her to act as a sexy, frivolous blond. Her career only showed a small aspect of her complex artistic personality. As a sensitive and smart person, she was also fond of poetry and wrote notes to herself along with poems. She used writing as an introspective tool to express a part of herself that could not find its place in front of a camera. Her writings have been published only recently under the title *Fragments* (2010)[*] after having been hidden for decades, probably in order not to ruin her established image.

Marilyn Monroe experienced fame in the 1950s at a time when women had not many possibilities to gain either independence or worldwide recognition outside of an actress's or a singer's career. And she mastered the two. Her sex appeal was widely acclaimed by society, but she paid the price for it. She kept feeling emotionally insecure throughout her life, which led her to a severe state of depression. This is only partly due to her difficult childhood. The thousands of pictures that reduced her to a pinup girl – literally a girl whose picture is pinned up on the bed's wall – certainly did not help her to feel whole. The cause of her death remains unexplained, but she was crushed by the world's demands to give more. Indeed, as a viewer, we encourage the demand for pictures that we look at, which increases their production.

Let women shine differently; let them shine elsewhere.

It is time to move beyond boundaries. We need to broaden our perception of women as well as of beauty. It will benefit

---

[*] Stanley Buchthal and Bernard Comment, *Fragments: Poems, Intimate Notes, Letters By Marilyn Monroe*, New York, Farrar, Straus and Giroux, 2010.

everybody, especially girls. A close look at pictures of men helps to see what's wrong with pictures of women; what guys are not requested to do should not be required by any woman in any picture. This includes: not wearing anything or almost anything, wearing a dress or a rock, wearing high heels or makeup. It should then be socially accepted that actresses, top models, and singers wear non-revealing clothes. If men do not need any sexy clothes and makeup to appear publicly, it should not be expected from women either. Women of all ages have the right to exist the way they are; they should not feel any need to enhance themselves with sexy clothes and makeup to get attention and be loved.

What a woman feels the inner need to do, like applying makeup or being sexy, has much to do with what she is expected to do.

Sex Appeal VS Intelligence

Our society is fond of artificiality, which lies in our strong taste for advanced technology and outer beauty. Today's pictures of women bring together the two: our love for polished images and our submission to women's physical appearance. Pictures have become shrines to celebrate the cult of women's beauty but only a certain kind of beauty. Are top models, actresses and singers the goddesses of today? For sure, their widespread images act as examples to guide other women, who further tend to mirror them. In a society like ours driven by pictures, it is no surprise that physical appearance matters now more than anything else. Outer beauty, and more particularly sex appeal, has become our greatest value. It is one of the reasons why intelligence, which is a key inner quality, is never considered when talking about a woman.

We overvalue women's physical appearance to the detriment of inner qualities such as intelligence, sense of humor, strength, and wisdom.

Our society devalues these inner qualities through pictures to shrink women.

Today's pictures emphasize even more than before women's outer qualities. It is not a secret for anyone that digital technology is used to trick and standardize women's body shapes to make them more appealing and catch the viewer's eyes instantly. Pretty much everything can be modified through digital technology: the shape of the eyes, lips, nose, and face, as well as the overall appearance of women, especially the texture of their skin, the size of their breasts, the shape of their hips, behind and legs. Add to that all the older tricks, such as makeup, high heels, hair coloring and extensions, wigs, false eyelashes and nails, nail polish, face and body hair removal, push-up bras and tights, face, and body plastic surgery. This is how the natural beauty of women is sold around the world. And it does not leave much room to display something else.

As a result, our perception of women as well as of women's beauty is crooked.

Men and boys are exhorted to love these pictures to be considered as true men, which reinforces the power of these depictions while lowering women's social status in society.

Valorizing Girls and Women's Inner Qualities

If women will exist suchlike for men's eyes in pictures and in daily life, women will not be considered equal to men. Indeed, women cannot be "seen" as equal to men. Being equal to men means to behave equally to them: nurturing one's intelligence and other inner qualities through education, readings, arts, sports, travels, and conversations. A well-balanced society also implies that both men and women valorize women's inner qualities, that we all encourage our daughters or granddaughters, wives, girlfriends, and co-workers to bring them out (see at the end of the book: "Some Ideas to Valorize Girls and Women's Inner Qualities"). This means to let girls and women speak and express themselves and finally to let them achieve what they want in their lives while supporting them. This will induce a completely different quality in pictures of women.

What Do I Think of Beauty as an Art Historian?

To me, beauty can be anywhere, in all shapes of nature as well as in human productions such as art, music, poetry or objects and behaviors. Its diversity makes it impossible to standardize in beauty standards and sum up in pictures. Water, trees, every single leaf, flowers, animals, and stones are astonishing masterpieces of nature; their infinite diversity of shapes, colors and patterns are echoing the infinite faces and body shapes of people around the planet. That's why it does not make sense, neither to establish beauty standards nor to trick our faces and bodies to fit them. The single thing we need to change is our own perception of beauty, which needs to be widely extended.

Nakedness itself is not indecent; the naked body is beautiful if it is respected, and if men along with women show up with grace or intelligence without selling themselves as a commodity (see in the "Pictures List" the documentary films about the dancer Anna Halprin and the artist Marina Abramović who both performed naked with men). The reverse is equally true; the clothed body is beautiful, and there is no problem to show women clothed just as much as men are. As our body and mind are interconnected, there is also no reason to consider that beauty only lays down on the skin surface. Inner qualities such as intelligence, sense of humor, strength and wisdom are as beautiful as our bodies.

A special note on wrinkles: today's depictions of eternal youth create beauty standards that no one can fulfil anymore, not even women performers who have to enhance their bodies with plastic surgery to keep matching them through the years. Wrinkles are considered as flaws in commercial photography and in the film industry. As a result, ageing frightens all women well before old age; even young girls are now scared to pass 17 and get older. Life is meant to be celebrated at any age; every woman should feel good about herself – her body, mind, and soul – no matter how old she is. Wrinkles are part of a natural process that should be acknowledged so. Then, instead of creams to fight years, why not advertise how to take care of our bodies and enrich our lives? Everybody will gain to consider life the way it is and then work on it.

Towards Fair and Inspiring Pictures of Women

Evolution matters, and as human beings, we are all concerned. Have you ever wondered what we all do today will one be day considered outdated? Pictures of women are one of these; we produce them, watch, and share them with others, and at the end, we accept them silently, which convinces every one of us that these pictures are perfectly okay, though they are not.

Once we will have moved forward, today's depictions of women will look archaic.

Other talented women and types of bodies, other skills that are required on stage can be emphasized by the media. We are now able to broadcast a whole bouquet of women's blossoming careers. Fictional and documentary films, interviews and talks, photographs, comics, graphic novels, and children's books dedicated to a broader range of women will bring the visibility that all girls and women deserve. Some actresses call up for more interesting female leading roles in cinema; actresses also want to widen women's standards. They want to play more main parts and thus more diverse and deeper ones. Actresses, singers, and top models have a right to be equitably depicted.

Women who carve their own lives and fulfil their personal needs and goals are our best role models, like philanthropists of all fields, volunteers, independent women, artisans, gardeners, spiritual leaders, humanitarians, scientists, explorers, writers, artists, environmental and social activists from around the world. It is a shame for our society that seniors are deprived of pictures. Like children, they are underrepresented because they do not fit the standards of society based on sex appeal. Just like people who have an out-of-standard body and transgender people. Elderlies are among the wisest; their life experience could guide so many others. The voices and hopes of girls matter as adult ones; they should be equally broadcast. We need to see more of inspirational girls and women like Malala, Simone de Beauvoir and Mother Teresa. We need to create pictures that are anchored in daily life and represent girls and women the way they truly are – the kind of pictures that not only invite them to show their natural look without enhancements (such as makeup, high heels, plastic surgery, digital retouching) but also valorize their inner qualities (intelligence, sense of humor, strength, and wisdom). In short, the kind of pictures that depict girls and women as whole, deep, and unique human beings. There is an urge to convey this diversity and embrace it through higher-quality pictures.

High-quality pictures deepen our understanding of the world, expand our viewpoint, and open new ways of thinking. They can be deeply inspirational. They are fair to everyone, including girls and women.

Such pictures do exist but are rare exceptions. We need to look for them to find them. At the end of this book, you will find a list of pictures that are close to this ideal thing, which I also describe more thoroughly below. It will guide those who want to invite girls and women to pose fairly and those who want to create female characters.

What Fair and Inspiring Pictures of Women Show

- Inspirational girls and women
- Their natural look without enhancements (such as makeup, high heels, hair coloring, false eyelashes and nails, nail polish, push-up bras and tights, plastic surgery, and digital retouching)
- Their inner qualities (intelligence, sense of humor, strength, wisdom)
    - Equality of men and women: Girls and women as protagonists (to reach a 50/50 shared with boys and men)
- Female performers are dressed or undressed as much as male singers, actors, top models are. Female characters as much as male characters.
- The diversity in terms of career, face and body shapes and age that exists in our society and in the world

A note on manga: Manga tends to idealize girls and women a lot. Standardized faces with big eyes do not depict Japanese girls and women's actual faces. Forever young-looking characters, occasionally depicted with extremely slender bodies and giant breasts, do not look like Japanese girls and women either; they do not look like any human beings.

Female characters with pink, purple and green hair have launched the same fashion among girls around the world who model what they see in pictures instead of being themselves. I advocate for fair and inspiring manga that depict realistic female characters of various ages as protagonists to build self-esteem in girls and women.

Producing Sustainable Pictures of Women

Our world is saturated with images of all kinds that are neither worthwhile nor sustainable. Climate change forces us to drastically reduce our human activities. It is imperative to reduce the production of pictures as well, which consumes an astronomical number of resources. We need to produce way fewer pictures and only meaningful, sustainable ones. They should be made either with second-hand resources or with natural and recyclable materials. Resources are precious; we need to use them wisely, only to produce a reasonable number of pictures of the best quality. So consciously made, pictures will be more sustainable. Fair and inspiring pictures of women are more sustainable than images of women mass-produced. As they do not require any unnecessary enhancements (makeup, high heels, hair coloring, false eyelashes and nails, nail polish, plastic surgery) made with harmful chemicals, these pictures are fairer to people and the planet.

Bringing Fair and Inspiring Pictures of Women Home

Our environment shapes us: our language, our knowledge, our behavior. Today's pictures of women form a large part of our environment; whether we like it or not, they impress us. If we cannot avoid staring at them on the streets and on the internet, we can, however, shape our home to reduce their impact. Children are particularly receptive to their environment, which their brains absorb it like a sponge to grow. Children usually pick up what is there, i.e., what they find in their surroundings: resources adults make available to them at home and outdoors (resorts, live events, films at the movie theatre). If girls and boys are surrounded by pictures of hot and standardized women performers, along with similar standardized toys like fashion and princess dolls, mermaid and fairy dolls and their depictions (cartoons, illustrated books, coloring books, posters, printed clothing, stickers), it is what boys and girls will experience of the world; these pictures and toys will shape their perception of life. Then, girls will look to model them in their daily lives. They may also soon feel deeply dissatisfied with themselves if they are not sized like them as sexy, beautiful, thin and, later in life, young as these women.

Pictures root powerful mental images that shape our way of seeing life.

Bonus A Game to Reflect on Pictures of Women That Surround Us

For men and women of all ages (from 5 years old). To play alone, with the family, with friends or with pupils in schools. Material:

- Pictures in your surroundings: still pictures on the internet, posters in your bedroom, front covers of magazines and books in your living room, advertisements on your way from home to work (or school) captured with a phone. For a child: cartoons, posters, illustrated books, coloring books, printed clothing, stickers.
- Clothes, shoes, makeup, etc. to borrow from your family, friends, or neighbors.

1. Pick a picture of a woman and a picture of a man. Pose these two pictures side by side and compare them: What are the main differences?

Possible answers: the woman is blond hair dyed, wears makeup, high heels, short or skinny clothes, a neckline, underwear, or no clothes at all. She shows obvious signs of plastic surgery to emphasize her lips, breasts or look younger. On the exact opposite, the man is bare-faced, his hair color is natural, he wears flat shoes and is dressed from neck to toes with loose clothes or topless (excessively muscular men only). He shows no obvious signs of plastic surgery.

Questions: Do you find these pictures fair? Do they show equality of women and men?

2. Pick two pictures of women. Pose these two pictures side by side and compare them: What are the main differences?

Possible answers: These pictures of women are not so different from each other; they have pretty much the same age, face, and body shapes, as well as skin color. Their hair color is also about the same (blond hair dyed), and they both wear makeup, revealing clothes and high heels. They both show obvious signs of plastic surgery.

Questions: Are these pictures fair to these two women? Are they fair to women and girl viewers? And to men and boy viewers?

3. If you are a boy/man, pick one picture of a woman. If you are a girl/woman, pick the picture of the man. Try to shoot an exact copy of it. If you are a boy/man, dress, shave, with a bra and two apples to fake breasts, high heels, makeup, etc., and pose like this woman. If you are a girl/woman, dress from neck to toes with loose clothes, flat shoes, a

> hairstyle as natural as possible, bare face, and pose like this man. Question: How does it feel to be depicted as a woman/man?
>
> 4. Now, take time to reflect on what you have learnt from this game. What have you discovered that you have not noticed before? How can you use this new knowledge in your daily life?
>
> Questions that might come to mind: Do I really need these pictures? Should I pay for that? Do I need these pictures to be of myself? Is there another kind of picture my family and I could look at, for example, the kind of picture that is fair and inspiring?

Then, it is our duty to support high-quality pictures of women that enhance ourselves and our families and to carefully select the TV shows, magazines, videos, as well as the films, books, video games, manga, comics, and children's books that surround us. At the movie theatre, we are also free to pick the films to which we expose ourselves and our family. Through the ages, our environment continues to mound our ideas; as for children and teenagers, it can narrow or broaden our understanding of the world. For this reason, we need to keep our minds open to a wide range of high-quality pictures to extend our perception of reality. What we pour in our body, mind and soul affects us. As much as a balanced diet feeds us properly, fair, and inspiring pictures of women can uplift our lives too (see below the "Pictures List" to bring such fair and inspiring pictures home). It does not only make a difference within ourselves and our families, it can also improve the quality of our social interactions and elevate our whole society.

Afterword

It is time to offer us, girls and boys, men and women, a wider range of pictures of women to broaden our perspectives and balance our viewpoints. This will bring more equality between men and women and then more harmony between all of us. Unlike the pictures misused to cyberbully girls, today's pictures of women should not be banned. Nevertheless, it is essential to think about the making of pictures outside of the box to frame women differently and then to produce a fresh renewal of images in terms of career, face and body shapes and age.

Pictures List
Fair and Inspiring
Pictures of Women

A few samples of fair and inspiring pictures of girls and women to watch and discuss in family, with friends, in schools or to offer as a present:

Online Talks

Maysoon Zayid, *I Got 99 Problems...Palsy Is Just One* (2013), TEDWomen 2013, TED Talk video. A talk given by an actress and a stand-up comic who advocates for people with disabilities, women, and Arabs with a great sense of humor.

Jade Hameister, *My Journey to the North Pole and Beyond* (2016), TEDxMelbourne, YouTube video. A talk by a 14-year-old explorer of the North Pole given to empower young women to pursue their dreams.

Chimamanda Ngozi Adichie, *The Danger of a Single Story* (2009), TEDGlobal 2009, TED Talk video. Chimamanda Ngozi Adichie is a writer who tells us a few personal stories about the danger of knowing only a single story.

Tracy McMillan, *The Person You Really Need to Marry* (2014), TEDxOlympicBlvdWomen, YouTube video. A talk given by a television author and a relationship expert who shares her life experience and wisdom.

Ruth Chang, *How to Make Hard Choices?* (2014), TEDSalon NY, 2014, TED Talk video. Ruth Change is a philosopher who studies how hard choices shape our lives and make us who we are.

Lee Mokobe, *A Powerful Poem About What It Feels Like to Be Transgender* (2015), TEDWomen 2015, TED Talk video. Lee Mokobe is a slam poet who explores gender identity through his own words and experience.

Jane Goodall, *What Separates Us from Chimpanzees* (2002), TED2002, TED Talk video. Jane Goodall is a primatologist, conservationist and humanitarian who speaks about respect for all life, hope and peace.

Dame Ellen MacArthur, *The Surprising Thing I Learned Sailing Solo Around the World* (2015), TED2015, TED Talk video. Dame Ellen MacArthur is a solo sailor who circled the globe and advocates for a more sustainable economy.

Diana Nyad, *Never, Ever Give Up* (2013), TEDWomen 2013, TED Talk video. A talk given by a long-distance swimmer who, at age 64, was the first person to swim from Cuba to Florida.

Greta Thunberg, *The Disarming Case to Act Right Now on Climate Change* (2018), TEDxStockholm, TED Talk video. Greta Thunberg is an environmental activist who raised awareness about climate change worldwide.

Kakenya Ntaiya, *A Girl Who Demanded School* (2012), TEDxMidAtlantic, TED Talk video. Kakenya Ntaiya is an educator and activist who built the first school for girls in her Maasai village in Kenya.

Sakena Yacoobi, *How I Stopped the Taliban From Shutting Down My School* (2015), TEDWomen 2015, TED Talk video. Sakena Yacoobi is an education activist who set up schools in secret throughout Afghanistan to provide teacher training to women and men.

Olga Murray, *What If You Could Live a Joyful and Vibrant Life at Any Age?* (2015), TEDxVienna, YouTube video. At age 65, Olga Murray founded an organization in Nepal that helped 45,000 children. She shares her story and wisdom to encourage others to live a joyful life.

Fine Brothers Entertainment, *Kids React to Gay Marriage Ruling* (2015), YouTube video.

When children discuss civil rights with a bright intellect.

Documentary Films

The Beaches of Agnès (2008), an autobiographical documentary film by Agnès Varda about her lifetime as an ever-inventive woman and filmmaker.

Breath Made Visible (2009), a documentary film by Ruedi Gerber about Anna Halprin's lifetime achievements as an innovative dancer and choreographer.

He Named Me Malala (2015), a documentary film by Davis Guggenheim about Malala Yousafzai, a bold 17-year-old girl winner of the Nobel Peace Prize.

Marina Abramović: The Artist Is Present (2012), a documentary film by Matthew Akers and Jeff Dupre about the breathtaking performance artist Marina Abramović, who had a retrospective at MoMA. This film shows provocative pictures of the woman's body that are not suitable for children.

Fictional Film

La Belle Verte (1996), a visionary film directed and played by Coline Serreau (French audio with English subtitles). See the DVD included in the book: Coline Serreau, *La Belle Verte*, Arles, Actes Sud, 2009. Coline Serreau plays a wise alien challenged by the Earth inhabitants' way of life, especially by their relationship to nature and, along the way, makeup.

Music Video Clip

Grace VanderWaal, *The A Team* (2017), Paste Studios, New York, 1/23/2017, YouTube video. Grace VanderWaal is a songwriter, singer, and ukulele player. This video is a cover of a song written by Ed Sheeran that expresses the struggles faced by a prostitute. The pictures reveal Grace VanderWaal's great sensitivity and intelligence, as well as her fair look.

Animation

The School of Life (in collaboration with Avi Ofer), *Why You Need an Early Night* (2017), YouTube video. *The School of Life* aims to develop emotional intelligence. This fair and inspiring video portrays the daily life of a woman who learns how to be wiser.

Illustrated Books

All the books listed below are excellent reads for all ages, including for younger children who can have them as bedtime stories. I chose them not only for their remarkable pictures but also for the message that they deliver. I privileged nonfiction books about role models, though the list also contains some outstanding fiction books that are fair and inspiring. I retained the children's books whose pictures are accurate; too often the drawings of children's books enhance the role models by changing their hair color from dark to blond, their eye color from brown to blue or by adding lipstick and nail polish, while the photographs of these women show that they wore none. Sometimes the shape of their faces is changed too to look thinner, or they suddenly wear a garment with a neckline. I kept the most fair and inspiring books.

For Adults and Teenagers

Lisa Congdon, *A Glorious Freedom: Older Women Leading Extraordinary Lives*, San Francisco, Chronicle Books, 2017. An illustrated book that portrays inspirational women from the past and today who bloomed over the age of 40. Along with profiles, interviews and essays, the book contains drawings of these older women made by the author.

From 8–10 Years Old

Katherine Halligan and Sarah Walsh, *Herstory: 50 Women and Girls Who Shook the World*, London, Nosy Crow, 2018. A book packed with photographs, illustrations, stories, and wise quotes that portrays 50 inspirational girls and women who changed world history: writers, artists, scientists, explorers, leaders, and activists.

From 5 Years Old

Kate Pankhurst, *Fantastically Great Women Who Changed the World*, London, Bloomsbury, 2016. An illustrated book that introduces 13 female role models of world history.

Picture Books

Laurie Lawlor and Laura Beingessner, *Rachel Carson and Her Book That Changed the World*, New York, Holiday House, 2012. This picture book is about the life of Rachel Carson, who was a marine biologist and pioneering environmentalist.

Claire A. Nivola, *Planting the Trees of Kenya: The Story of Wangari Maathai*, New York, Farrar, Straus and Giroux, 2008. This picture book is about the life of Wangari Maathai, an environmentalist winner of the Nobel Peace Prize who saved the natural environment and the people in Kenya.

Patrick McDonnel, *Me...Jane*, New York, Little Brown Books for Young Readers, 2011. A picture book about the young Jane Goodall, who dreamt of living with and helping animals and later became a revered primatologist, conservationist and humanitarian.

Children's Fiction Books

Christina Björk and Lena Anderson have created a series of three books around Linnea, a lively girl who loves life, plants and nature:

- *Linnea in Monet's Garden*, Naperville, Sourcebooks Jabberwocky, 2012.
- *Linnea's Almanac*, R&S Books, 1989.
- *Linnea's Windowsill Garden*, R&S Books, 1988[*].

Roald Dahl, *Matilda*, illustrated by Quentin Blake, London, Penguin Random House, 2016. Matilda is a brilliant and sensitive five-year-old child who loves books and taught herself to read. His fascination for Mozart, who was already composing music when he was five years old, led the author, Roald Dahl, to create this brilliant female character.

Graphic Novels

Marjane Satrapi, *The Complete Persepolis*, New York, Pantheon Books, 2007. *Persepolis* is a graphic memoir by Marjane Satrapi about her childhood and early adult years in Iran. The author depicts herself as a strong, rebel and anti-authoritarian female character.

Liz Prince, *Tomboy*, San Francisco, Zest Books, 2014. This graphic memoir by Liz Prince is about her childhood and adolescence as a tomboy. The author explores what it means to grow up female with humor and frankness. This book contains a few curse words, as Liz Prince experienced bullying.

---

[*] Though this book is of the best quality, one of its double pages advises to use smoke to kill bugs. It is important to explain to children that we know now that smoking is toxic and can cause cancer. To keep away insects, we use environmentally friendly products today instead of smoke.

Philippa Rice, *Soppy*, Kansas City, Andrews McMeel Publishing, 2014. *Soppy* is a comic by Philippa Rice based on real-life moments with her boyfriend. This book is about true love, small gestures and the beauty of everyday life.

For Further Fair and Inspiring Pictures

The staff of your local library, bookstore and movie theatre can guide you for further documentary films and books about girls and women if you ask them.

- TED Talks videos: https://www.ted.com/
- Documentary film festivals

A great way to connect with high-quality pictures of women is to attend a documentary film festival for a weekend. Here are some major ones:

AFI DOCS Film Festival, Silver Spring (near Washington, D.C., US)

Full Frame Documentary Film Festival, Durham (North Carolina, US)

Hot Docs, Toronto (Canada)

Sheffield Doc/Fest, Sheffield (UK)

- Documentary films, autobiographies and memoirs

Documentary films about women as well as women's written autobiographies and memoirs, which sometimes include photographs on the front cover and inside the book, offer insightful views on women's lives. They can be chosen according to one's personal taste for sports, arts, history, politics and science or picked up randomly to discover something new and extend one's perception of women. Some remarkable books are Simone de Beauvoir's *Memoirs of a Dutiful Daughter* (1958), Helen Keller's *The Story of My Life* (1903) and Anne Frank's *The Diary of a Young Girl* (1947).

Some Ideas to Valorize Girls and Women's Inner Qualities (Intelligence, Sense of Humor, Strength and Wisdom):

1. Letting girls and women speak and express themselves

   – At home (during meals) and at work (during meetings and meals). If it does not come spontaneously, ask girls and women for their opinions, feelings, ideas, hopes and respect them as much as possible.

   – Freedom to be themselves, love and care allow girls and women to blossom. Taking time to listen to their needs and seeking to understand them when something goes wrong are essential.

2. Supporting girls and women's choices and life dreams

   – Providing them with a good education and continuing education that touches their self-interest. A child-based education is ideal to start in life (see the reading list for further information).

– Providing girls with a learning environment with various resources to support their exploration of the world (broaden their knowledge) and fuel their passion (deepen their knowledge):

What is a passion? It is often free play(s) or activity(ies) children and teenagers love doing and what they keep doing once they are adults. It is then essential to let children and teenagers play freely as much as they want while providing them with resources that touch on their self-interest. What they choose to do by themselves is best for them if they do not hurt themselves or somebody else, including animals and nature. A **library card** is a passport for life; it is one of the first presents to offer to a child as it gives them free access to a wide variety of resources. The list of resources provided below is not exhaustive; it is meant to give an overview. One way to use it is to read it aloud to children and teenagers and list what they would love to try at least once.

We are the first role models for our children. Let's use environmentally friendly products, second-hand resources, as well as organic and recyclable materials.

Free time: Unstructured free plays that children invent are as essential for their development as organized activities. They are unique to each child and pop up spontaneously when children have free time and are not directed. Free time is also important to relax and do nothing.

Home activities: drawing, cooking, cleaning home together with the boys and dads, recycling, making a garment from old clothes, listening to or playing music, dancing, writing a diary, a story, a poem, writing and singing a song, writing and playing a play, looking at a desktop world globe, leafing through an atlas of world wildlife or a human body encyclopedia, making a video, taking photographs, organizing an event in the neighborhood, surfing the internet, collecting information on a favorite topic, listening to a bedtime story or a classic book.

Outdoor activities: walking in nature, observing wildlife, watching a sunrise, looking at the stars, building a hut, making an ephemeral sculpture (stone balancing, a snowman), planting a tree, growing vegetables, identifying edible plants (nettles, dandelion), reading the clouds to predict the weather, going camping.

Books, magazines and films from the library

Talks and lectures: online and "live" about topics such as environmental and social current issues, health and food, human rights and the rights of living things, religions, personal growth, earth and life sciences, history, arts, literature, philosophy and psychology.

Classes and social clubs: first-aid training, sports, dance, yoga, meditation, handicrafts, science, arts, languages.

Nonprofit organizations: joining a peace march, volunteering to protect nature or a favorite animal, helping people in their home city or around the world.

Museums, live shows and festivals: art, documentary film, photography, comics, poetry, stand-up comedy, theatre, opera, dance, music, science, history, sports.

Travelling in a home city and its surroundings, or backpacking abroad using trains, bicycles or feet, to discover other landscapes, people, cultures and languages.

Conversations with people from various ages and backgrounds (speaking with people, staying at a hosteling international hostel).

3. Promoting our inner qualities:

   – Giving free compliments to girls and women to acknowledge their intelligence, sense of humor, strength and wisdom and to acknowledge their achievements.
   – Providing girls and boys information about role models: documentary films, talks, interviews, autobiographies, or books role models conceived as authors (see "The Pictures List" for pictures of girls and women). For boys and men role models, see Jon Jandai, Sam Berns, Paul McCartney, Thich Nhat Hanh, Henry David Thoreau, Gandhi, Nelson Mandela and Matthieu Ricard, among others.

- "Classics" written by role models to enrich our inner lives:
- Mother Teresa, *No Greater Love* (1997)
- Thich Nhat Hanh, *How to Love* (2015)
- Gandhi, *An Autobiography or the Story of My Experiments with Truth* (1927)
- Marshall B. Rosenberg, *Nonviolent Communication: A Language of Life* (1999)
- Etty Hillesum, *An Interrupted Life: The Diaries 1941–1943* (1981)
- Louise Hay, *You Can Heal Your Life* (1984)

4. Honoring our natural bodies through:

- A message to spread: "Your body is perfect the way it is" or "I prefer you without make-up and high heels" or "I love your natural hair".
- Healthy food and water as a drink (homemade meals that include fresh food from the organic farmers' market).
- Some physical activities: walking in nature, cycling, gardening, dancing or swimming
- Other natural cares: meditation, yoga, sauna, massages, natural products to clean the body and the house
- Something to try once: a life-drawing class or a contemporary dance class to take notice of the infinite variety of the human face and body shapes and see that they are all fine.

5. Making fair and inspiring pictures of women:

Making few pictures, but of the best quality, meaningful pictures made sustainably.

Documentary and fictional films, photography about girls and women role models that invite them to show their natural look without enhancements (such as make-up, high heels, hair coloring, false eyelashes and nails, nail polish, push-up bras and tights, plastic surgery and digital retouching).

Children's books and films, comics and graphic novels based on girls and women role models' lives. Fictions with intelligent, funny, strong and wise female leading characters whose stories are anchored in daily life and could be true (without princesses, mermaids, fairies and superheroes with magical powers). Essential themes to depict are: how to protect the environment, how to solve conflicts through nonviolent communication, how to make friendships last and build stable relationships, how to take care of our body and mind. Female characters dressed as much as male characters are.

Music video clips, **fictional films and commercial photography** that show girls and women's inner qualities (intelligence, sense of humor, strength, wisdom) and their natural look without enhancements. Dressed or undressed as much as men are.

Producing and broadcasting pictures of a wide range of women in terms of career, face and body shapes and age in which inspirational girls and women have leading roles.

Appendix

On Older Pictures and Art History

Today's depictions of women are rooted in the past. Older pictures, such as paintings, already show an imbalance between men and women. This imbalance starts going crescendo with Rococo (XVIIIe siècle), where we see more and more nude women and fewer and fewer nude men. It culminates in the nineteenth century with one of the most iconic artworks painted by Manet, *The Luncheon on the Grass* (1863), which presents a nude woman in front of two men, both dressed from neck to toes. Like those of today, naked men were once represented as very muscular, in a position of strength, especially when abducting women (Pierre-Paul Rubens, *The Rape of the Daughters of Leucippus*, 1618). Works of art associated with rape and domination should be questioned and relegated to the stacks in favor of fair artworks. Pictures exhibited in museums and reproduced in art books are valued by the art world. The art world is responsible for what it shows to the public. This raises the following questions: What works do we want to present to children and their families? What images do we want to promote and circulate within society?

Some tips:

– Find a balance between nude and clothed depictions of the woman body. For example, *The Luncheon on the Grass* by Manet could be exhibited beside or on the opposite wall of Paula Rego's *The Artist in Her Studio* (1993) to offer a counterpoint to viewers, or it could also be shown together with a sculpture of a nude man.

– Favor artworks that match our current values: Exhibit fair works of art and take others off the wall: Pierre-Paul Rubens, *The Rape of the Daughters of Leucippus* (1618) and Jean-Léon Gérôme, *A Roman Slave Market* (1884) are both unacceptable. In the past, our ancestors had their own tastes and ways of thinking. We have the right to part to make our own choices according to changes in society and what we want to value.